Little but
VICTORIOUS
Devotional

Little but VICTORIOUS Devotional

ELISHA PEREZ

XULON PRESS

Xulon Press
2301 Lucien Way #415
Maitland, FL 32751
407.339.4217
www.xulonpress.com

Paperback ISBN-13: 978-1-6628-2720-4
eBook ISBN-13: 978-1-6628-2721-1

Dedication

To my eldest son Jessie thank you, my life has been made more beautiful the day God blessed me with you. Although life has brought us much sorrow and lessons learned, it also has brought on a multitude of great joy an experience I will never forget. Son learning you has been the highlight of my life, as I learned myself, I become a better mother and woman of God. All I ever prayed for was to be someone that you could look up to and be proud of just as you have made me proud. You inspire me to want more and do better. I am so proud to call you my son and I am so excited for the young man you are an are becoming in Christ Jesus. You are a wonderful big brother patient and kind loving and inspirational your brother and I are blessed to have you. You are an amazing son, and I could not ask for a better firstborn. God bless you and keep you forever and always and thank you for always being a warm hug in a culture that has always been cold.

To the Highlight of my days, my baby boy Brandon; You put a smile on my face just with a thought of you, you have taught me so much. I know you are God sent just for me He placed you in my life at just the right time, although you came two months early. God brought you in my life to teach me patience, I learned a different way to love because of how you love and how uncon-ditional you are with your kindness and love everyone. You view the world so beautifully with just excitement and appreciation, you taught me to pause and look at the creators work the same way and I appreciate the beauty in the world so much more now. God has giving you a Spirit that lights up the darkest room with just a smile. You hug everyone physically and spiritually. You remind me of who I used to be before I was conformed by the world. So, I am thankful that God uses the Holy Spirit to work in you to remind me that God is always near, with your random shouts of praise when it's so quite you could hear a pin drop and my thoughts are being consumed you give a shout of "Hallelujah Jesus! God is Good! And a Glory to God!" I am immediately inspired and uplifted. I thank you so much although you are young now one day, I pray you realize that you have taught me more then I believe I could teach at the age of six.

I heard or read somewhere that God blesses women with sons to teach women how to be loved, I do not know how true that is but what I do know is that learning to love Christ for my sons opened my eyes to how much they loved me and its uncondi-tional just has Jesus loved us, so in a sense I do believe that logic. So, to my sons I pray that your love is forever changing and growing in the Lord, know that I will forever love you as Christ loves all his children, although life will come at you fast every-thing works together for the good of those who love Christ. Continue being the men of God that He has called you to be. I dedicate this book to you.

Acknowledgments

To the kingdom women in my life my grandma Lydia Cosme, you made it a point to always keep me in church instilling in me the word of God at a young age. Even though life's circumstances and trials kept me away from God for a long time, I choose to keep God close to my heart because of your lessons and your faithfulness you are an inspiration to me, a powerful and wonderful woman of God. I honor all that you are and all that you have been to me because I know it was your prayers continually interceding for me. I thank you and I love you mom Cosme. To my spiritual mother prophetess Carmen Robinson and Sister in Christ Alysia Thurman, thank you for accepting myself and my family as part of your family we thank you. Your hearts are so genuine and full of love, your arms completely open for the body of Christ you are both wonderful victorious women of God. Thank you for allowing the Holy Spirit to move within you to be laborers in my life. Thank you for the inspiration and continual encouragement to pursue my godly purpose. You both have been a blessing in my life and in my children's lives, and I am proud to not only be a part of a family in Christ but also a sisterhood in the Lords eyes fulfilling God's purpose for the kingdom. I prayed for such a bond as this, I am honored that you call me daughter and sister, I love you both and am grateful for the love you pour out to me and my family. I am glad to be walking in fellowship with the both of you and I am excited for the works we will be doing for the people of God. May God continue to bless you and keep you covered with the blood of Jesus.

To Pastor Brian Robinson the inspirational leader of our church and Family, I thank God for the calling on your life, I thank you for submitting yourself to Gods will and purpose for your life also allowing the spirit of the Lord to dwell in you, I give God thanks for using you to share the word and revelation in a way that only God can. You are a righteous man of God and you have given an example of what a man of God is and should be, your faithfulness and dedication to your wife prophetess Carmen Robinson, the family physical, and spiritual children, and to AFKGM Church are unmeasurable and I am eternally honored and grateful to be a member of this kingdom family.

I would like to also thank AFKGM (Anointed for Kingdom Ministry) family and everyone that I have encountered before and or during my walk in Christ, a lot of my life and purpose is a result of the contribution that many of you both indirectly and directly helped mold me into the woman of God that I am today by encouragement, inspiration, by life lessons and experiences, with wisdom and giving knowledge of God and simply just accepting me, for whom I was, whom I am now and whom I will be in my walk with the Lord. I thank you.

Introduction

There came a time when I just became tired of life, drained, and fed up even. Where was my life going? What was my purpose? Why did God bring me this far and why am I still struggling mentally, emotionally, physically, and spiritually?

If you have asked yourself any of those questions, then you picked up the right book!

I uprooted my family clear across the east coast from Pennsylvania to the southern state of Florida, I had no one I could depend or rely on but ironically that's where God does His best work. Ever noticed that? My mind was in a battle with everything, and my heart was feeling the effects of it. Physically I was drained, mentally I felt defeated and spiritually I felt abandoned.

Are you tired yet?

Well in my tiredness I learned that I have power over my mind, I have power over my heart, power over my body, and my spirit just needed to be strengthened by the word of God to activate these powers. Have you ever had a friend or family member give you a word and it just uplifts you? I am here to tell you; you can find that encouragement in the bible. A book of the word of God created just for your every situation for your very circumstance, a guide to help you through it all, filled with encouraging scriptures to get you through the trial's life throws at you. There was nothing more comforting or more important than learning that there was a purpose-filled life plan set out for me and a renewing in me waiting to breakthrough and I just needed to submit to God and his word. Be encouraged your time is not up yet but the enemies time is.

Prepare Your Mind

$$\sim\!\!\infty\!\!\sim\!\!\infty\!\!\sim$$

Joshua 1:8

This book of the law shall not depart from your mouth, but you shall meditate in it day and night, that you may observe to do according to all that is written in it. For then you will make your way prosperous and then you will have good success.

Ephesians 4:23

And be renewed in the spirit of your mind.

Matthew 22:37

Jesus said, "you shall love the Lord your God with all your heart with all your soul with all your mind."

Pray over distractions if there is anything not allowing you to focus on God,

Make a list of those things!

Now let us pray,

Heavenly father I come to you with a humbled heart wanting to meditate on your word, so I ask that you bind up every spiritual distraction of and from (insert above list) your word reminds me that I have the power in my mouth to ask anything of you and it shall be according to your will Father. For I am the head and not the tail and as you go before me in all things Lord, I ask you to go before me right now, I pray that you remove all distractions and anything that is not of you from me right now, so as I move forward in reading your word today, I can be filled with the spirit of your truth. In your mighty name Jesus, I pray,

Amen.

Refer to this prayer and revise your list as needed.

Meditation and Prayer

Mark 1: 35
Now in the morning having risen a long while before daylight, He went out and departed to a solitary place and there He prayed.

Do you have a solidary place and time to get away from the world and get closer to God?

Where is it?

When is your devotional time?

Writing out these places and a scheduled time will help with developing a strong foundation with the Lord and help make you accountable for that time. Write out your committed and dedicated places and times down.

What is your prayer relationship like now?

How would you like to see your relationship with God grow? Write your goals down...

John 14: 6
Jesus said to him, "I am the way, the truth, and the life, no one comes to the Father except through Me. If you had known me, you would have known my Father also; And from now on you have seen Him."

Romans 15:6
That you may with one mind and one mouth glorify the God and father of our Lord Jesus Christ.

Ask and You Shall Receive!

James 1: 6
But let him ask in faith, with no doubting. For he who doubts is like a wave of the sea driven and tossed.

After reading this passage, where is your faith?

Is it lacking somewhere?

Do you have doubts when asking God for something?

Why?

2 Timothy 1: 7
For God has not given us a spirit of fear, but of power and love and of a sound mind.

This passage should help give you peace of mind. Timothy writes about the power we have over our minds and our emotions.

How do you feel?

Do you still have lack in your faith or have any doubt in your mind over what you are asking for in Jesus' name?

James 4: 7
Therefore, submit to God resist the devil and he will flee from you.

We have all heard the saying "The mind is a terrible thing to waste." What if I told you that, that is not anymore truer for a believer and or follower of Christ? Resisting the devil is not only a physical temptation but also a mental one, I will dig deeper into that, doubt comes from the enemy, Sin, bad habits, confusion, distractions, etc. All to get you detoured from your purpose that God has set out for you. It is no coincidence that anytime you want to do anything regarding God like reading the bible, going to church, or even doing something good for someone or anything positive with a Godly mindset you get a mental battle of distraction, confusion, or temptation to do something sinful to pull you away from what you originally have set out to do in accordance with God's plan. So, when James states submit to God and the devil will flee, he is speaking mentally, physically, and spiritually to submit to God daily, because every day is going to be a new battle that the enemy is going to strategize against you and God's purpose for you.

Where do you believe the enemy has come against you in your relationship with God?

Submit it to God below and meditate with God about it and allow the Holy Spirit to guide your way and guard your path.

Let us Pray!

Matthew 6:9
This, then, is how you should pray:

"Our Father in heaven hallowed be Your name, Your Kingdom comes Your will be done, on earth as it is in heaven give us this day Our Daily Bread and forgive us our debts as we also forgive our debtors and lead us not into temptation but deliver us from the evil one for Yours is the Kingdom and the power and the glory.

Amen

His Grace

Joshua 1:9
Have I not commanded you? "Be strong and of good courage, do not be afraid. Nor be dismayed for the Lord your God is with you wherever you go."

James 1:3
Knowing that the testing of your faith produces patience.

Ephesians 2:8
For it is by grace you have been saved. Through faith, and this is not from yourself, it is the gift of God. Not by works so that no one can boast.

These passages help us to know that we should be encouraged and have faith although we may be "Tried we will not be Touched" for we are saved by God's grace because of our faith.

Meditate on these verses what sticks out to you?

How do you feel empowered?

2 Peter 1:2

Grace and peace be multiplied to you in the knowledge of God and of Jesus Christ our Lord.

Philippians 4:13

I can do all things through Christ who strengthens me.

Time out: Thank God right now for his Love, grace, and mercy!

Prepare Yourselves!

Romans 12: 2
Do not conform any longer to the pattern of this world. But let God transform you into a new person by changing the way you think.

How does this passage affect you? Or how will it affect you?

Are you scared of something?

Scared of what people will think? Or say?

Maybe your scared of how people will take the new you?

I had similar questions I knew this new walk of life would bring a lot of loss, death to the old me meant "no more" to a lot of things, no more drinking, no more smoking, no more hanging out in old places that would take me back to the old fleshly desires and no more temporary sexual satisfaction. I knew I had to distance myself from familiar people that would try to pull me away from my purpose. Although these things were all familiar and convenient, I was willing to give them up with no problem, again I told you I was tired of being tired. Using drugs, alcohol, and sex to numb up or fill a void I thought I had.

Nothing prepared me for the loss of friends and the distancing of family members. It was harder to talk to anyone living outside the will of God, every conversation or advice reverted to the word of God for me and most people living outside his will reverted to culture and their ways or as my pastor would call it "excuseology" yes, I know it's not a word, but it should be, some people rather live a life founded by excuses than to deal with the reality and the accountability of their circumstance. So, they become professionals at making excuses, some go as far as to blame God." Like why God would, etc.?" without taking accountability for their role and choices in the life they choose to live. See following God and being obedient is a choice as much as it is not to obey the will of the Father. I learned quickly that some are not on the same level spiritually and that is OK, they simply were not tired enough yet! My purpose as a follower of Christ was to present the word to them be a witness of his grace and mercy on my life. It is up to them how they interpret it and what they did with the word after. In **Deuteronomy 30:3** it says, "*Your God will restore everything you lost; he will have compassion on you, and he'll come back and pick up the pieces from all* *the places where you were scattered."* So, it is no coincidence that even though I have lost common interest with some friends and family members, I have gained fellowship relationships with those of like-mindedness.

Meditate on your answers.

"Prepare yourselves a new mind for the Lord your God will speak."

Maybe there are some people you already feel estranged with, just pray over them, and love them. Because above all else, it is what God asks of us, to love one another. I pray you already have some like-minded friends around you, rejoice in them and talk to them about concerns you may have and pray together for God's word says *"Among the proud, there are always contentions: but they that do all things with counsel are ruled by wisdom";* **Proverbs 13:10.** Humble yourself and seek counsel when needed about those relationships but not with anyone and everyone, ask God to bring people around you that are abiding in the word to help you pray through these situations. Let the Holy Spirit guide you into these new fellowship relationships.

Knowing His Word

Proverbs 3: 6
In all your ways acknowledge him, and he shall direct your paths.

Malachi 3: 6-7
For I am the Lord I do not change, return to me, and I will return to you.

2 Timothy 3:16-17
All scripture is given by inspiration of God and is profitable for doctrine for reproof, for correction, for instruction in righteousness. that the man of God may be complete thoroughly equipped for every good work.

Philippians 4: 6-7
Be anxious for nothing, but in everything by prayer and supplication with Thanksgiving, let your request be made known to God and the peace of God which surpasses all understanding will guard your hearts and minds through Christ Jesus.

Is there a path you thought you were supposed to take or maybe still do but got detoured along the way by culture or society's view of things?

Did you depart from God by trying to find your own way? How did you suffer?

Return to God meaning in His word and prayer cast your worries to Him. Without worry ask God to show you the path in which you should go according to what you have felt after reading these passages. Allow yourself to be led by the Holy Spirit at this time. Give yourself some quiet time to think about how God is directing you. Your relationship with God is so important currently so take as long as you need.

The Armor

Now that you have meditated on some of his words, it is time you suit up and get ready for battle. *"For we do not fight against the flesh and blood enemies but against authorities, against the powers over this present darkness, against the spiritual forces of evil in the heavenly places"*. ***Ephesians 6:12***

Imagine yourself getting ready for battle, suit up with the following,

The armor of God as it is found in ***Ephesians 6:14***

- *The belt of truth*
- *The breastplate of righteousness*
- *Your feet firm with the readiness of the gospel of peace*
- *The shield of faith*
- *The sword of the spirit powered with the word of God.*
- *The helmet of Salvation*

Now that you are ready how do you feel being a part of God's army, like David when he went up against Goliath, I hope!

His Word!

Philippians 4:4
Rejoice in the Lord always.

Ephesians 2:10
We are God's handiwork.

Ephesians 6: 18
Pray in the spirit on all occasions with all kinds of prayers and requests.

Isaiah 58: 10
Then you will call, and the Lord will answer, you will cry for help, and he will say: "Here I am!"

2 Corinthians 12: 9
My grace is sufficient for you, for My power is made perfect in weakness."

How great is it to rejoice and give God praise for all that he has done and is continually doing in us? We are His handiwork. Always pray to Him, He says because when you call, he will answer His grace is sufficient. When we are weak, he makes us strong. That may sound like a cliché to some, but it is so true. How many times have you prayed? And not the "God please let this light turn green" when traffics at a standstill prayer. Although it could be that simple sometimes, when have you poured out your heart to God in prayer and put all your faith and trust in Him?

How did you feel afterward?

Empowered?

Encouraged?

Enlightened?

At peace?

Is there a time you can think of? God answered your prayer and you immediately thought WOW this was God! Write that time down.

It is so easy to forget how far God has brought us when the enemies distracting us with attacks, that is why it is so important to meditate in His word and write down what He has brought you through and the blessings He has given you. Take this moment and bask in His glory, honor, and provisions and give Him praise for all He has done and is doing.

Faithfulness

2 Timothy 4:17-18
The Lord stood with me and strengthened me, so that the message might be preached fully through me and that all the Gentiles might hear Also, I was delivered out of the mouth of the lion and the Lord will deliver me from every evil work and preserve me for His heavenly Kingdom. To him be glory forever and ever. Amen!

Paul speaks about being delivered from the mouth of lions. Lions in this passage referring to trials and enemies because of his walk with Christ Jesus, brought on questions due to his past participation in the persecution of early disciples of Jesus. He would come across a lot of attacks, but he would not allow himself to be moved by these tribulations but was strengthen by God who continually delivered him so that he can do the will of God. Paul's life is a lot like some of ours, now of course we do not persecute Christians, but the life he lived before salvation, he was an unbeliever and doubted the works of Jesus and his disciples. Until Jesus opened his eyes. Well rather, he closed them for three days. Jesus blinded Paul for the unrighteousness done to his people. If you do not know Paul's story, I encourage you to read it. He was not one of the 12 disciples but was a particularly important part of the gospel of Christ. So, like Paul, you may not have always believed or understood the relationship with Jesus and why people followed, or maybe you always known about Him but never had a relationship with Him. Paul's story is a great example of the rebirth of the old man to the new man.

Is there a time you ever felt persecuted for something you knew to be right only to learn later you were taught wrong or informed wrongly?

How did that make you feel?

Some who are not living in the will of God would be angry, ashamed, want to blame someone else, or even deny the accusations like Peter denied knowing Jesus, not Paul he took responsibility for all he had done, repented, and followed Christ wholeheartedly and he brought other believers to the faith wherever he went he taught the word of God. Isn't that awesome? That God could transform even a murderer, a man so full of hate for the Lord, his people, and the works they were doing. Jesus turned his life completely around to bring others to the word of God.

Where are you on this walk?

What type of transformation are you needing?

How are you going to make these changes in your life?

Are you committed to this change?

The Law

Ephesians 4:29
Let no corrupt word proceed out of your mouth, but what is good for necessary edification. That it may impart grace to the hearers.

Ephesians 5:4
Neither filthiness, nor foolishness talking, nor course jesting, which are not fitting but rather giving of thanks.

It is easy to say I want to change but the reality is it is difficult to consistently submit to change, but God ensures us that he walks with us through it all, He will not allow us to bear more than we can handle. I do not know about you but that inspires me to want to seek him more abundantly. We talked about changing the way we think by meditating in His word. But what about the way we speak? It is so easy to have an unfiltered tongue. Especially in this culture when it has been normalized to use profanity, a joke at other's expense, talk perversely or simply talk foolishly.

I was one of those people. I had to teach myself to think, process, and then speak because I would speak with profanity knowingly and unknowingly, I wasn't completely fouled mouth but it wasn't Godly, I'd make jokes about people laugh at their expense sometimes, even jokingly be perverse, there's a saying that goes "you are what you eat", Well I'd like to change that to "we are how we speak" to be honest I didn't like that look on me, I was perverted, I was foolish, I was a joke, I was corrupt. And that's how others viewed me as well. I get less attention from people walking outside the will of God now and have less of a following but that is okay by me because how could I expect God's words to dwell on my tongue when it was full of filth? Their entertainment was no longer my priority. In Ephesians, we learn the laws of how we should speak.

How does this resonate with your life and how you speak?

Are there words that you have a hard time removing from your vocabulary? List them.

Imagine that someone targeted you or your family about something you were sensitive about how would that affect your self-esteem?

Is there someone or a group of people you make jokes about thinking it was harmless? Make a list of the people you may have hurt consciously or unconsciously even if they did not hear you. Reflect & repent about it here...

Take this time to check yourself and how you can improve in these areas,

If you are on the receiving end of the joke or foolish talking how has that made you feel? Can you forgive?

Whichever end your character is leaning toward give it to God and make peace with it for now you placed it in His hands, and you are renewed.

Be Renewed

John 7:38
"He who believes in me as the scripture has said, out of his heart will flow rivers of living water."

Psalm 51:10
Create in me a clean heart, O God, and renew a steadfast spirit within me.

Proverbs 4:23
"Above all else guard your heart for everything you do flows from it."

Your heart which consists of cardiac muscle is said to be the hardest working muscle in the body. So, it is safe to say, "it takes a licking and keeps on ticking!" medically and biblically speaking the Heart takes on the most challenges, Love, forgiveness, Hurt, pain, desires, etc. all things flow through this muscle, so it is no wonder Jesus says, "guard your heart" and in **Psalms 51:10**, it states to *"Create in me a clean heart"*. At times we hold on tight to hurt, pain, suffering, discouragement, and disappointment, all things the enemy uses against us to hold on to, in order to keep us in a state of depression and torment but letting go of these things help us to grow, prosper, and evolve so we do not fall into the same traps. It is ok to feel hurt and pain for a moment, so we are made stronger by working through it. We are not however meant to stagnate in our emotions of hurt, so much so it affects our life and output on it and others.

We are like soil needing to be watered continually to produce fresh flowers, fresh fruits, fresh produce. Now if our hearts are dried up from the pain, hurt, suffering, torment, and fill with disappointment, how can we pour out living water to ourselves and others? We cannot! We are made into weeds and what do weeds do they spread like wildfire not only around you but on other people's land.

Have you ever been around a negative person and no matter the advice you give or the environment they found a reason to be a "daffy downer" or a "negative person"? or been around someone sad? Heard a sad song? Watch a sad movie? Or a movie filled with violence? I am sure we all have experienced one or all of these.

How contagious were these emotions? Think of a time you were infected by any one of those emotions.

Is there a feeling of hurt or pain, maybe a lost loved one's grief you are holding on to?

Our emotions tie into our heart so much even after we fix our minds on something else, our heart remembers those feeling and if we allow it, it will consume us. So, guard your heart daily, submit it to God ask for the restoration of your heart and your mind before moving forward with your day starting right now.

Pray this with me,

Father God, I come to you submitting myself to you, humbling myself asking that before I move forward with my day, that you restore the broken pieces of my heart and renew my mind, I know that everything I do flows from it and I only want rivers of living waters to flow through me, guide me today, so I can guide and direct someone else in there a moment of despair, help me to steadfast on your word Lord, I am forgiving and letting go of all pain and hurt and any spirit the enemy has placed on me to keep me from healing right now in the name of Jesus Christ, I'm allowing the Holy Spirit to guide and direct my steps today according to your good and perfect will God. I thank you and honor you, Jesus in your mighty name I pray. Amen

Let This Sink In!

Psalm 46:10
Be still, and know that I am God, I will be exalted among the nations, I will be exalted in the earth.

Exodus 14:14
The Lord will fight for you, you need only to be still.

Mark 4:39
"Peace, be still!"

I know that there have been so many times I have tried to take care of things on my own, especially in relationships that I knew were not good for my wellbeing and had no Godly purpose in my life but still, I wanted it to work out, even after God had given me signs to let go. OUCH! That pain is something different, would you not agree?

Spending my days & nights crying wondering what was wrong with me praying to God to make it work meanwhile, not thinking Him not allowing it to work out WAS! Him making it work out. Hallelujah Jesus! There are so many scriptures in the bible that Jesus instructs us to "Be still". But because we are in a Burger King culture "having it your way, fast"! We have become impatient and want what we want when we want it, not thinking of the long-term damage this temporary fulfillment is going to cost. God allows us to go through what we want, to learn that it is not always what we need. He will fight for us, He will give us peace in any situation, and He will give us the desires of our hearts according to his will, but he does not want us to suffer to get it. There is a peace that comes when we learn to trust and have faith in God. Be still my child he is saying.

Is there a person, place, or thing God is telling you to be still? Write it down and maybe it is multiple things that come to mind, list them below, and do not be discouraged, imagine releasing it to God and allowing Him to have His way with it. And thank Him for how He is blessing you in this current situation or situations.

Thy Will Be Done

Mark 11:22-24

"Have faith in God" for assuredly, I say to you whoever says to this mountain: Be removed and be cast into the sea. and does not doubt in his heart but believes that those things he says will be done. He will have whatever he says. Therefore, I say to you. Whatever things you ask when you pray, believe that you receive them, and you will have them.

Proverbs 3:5

Trust in the Lord with all your heart, and lean not on your own understanding.

Psalms 37:7-9

Be still before the Lord. And wait patiently for him; Fret not yourself over the one who prospers in his way, because of the man who brings wicked schemes to pass, cease from anger and forsake wrath. Do not fret, it only causes harm. For evildoers shall be cut off; But those who wait on the Lord, they shall inherit the earth.

John 6:63

It is the spirit who gives life; the flesh profits nothing. The words that I speak to you are the spirit and they are life.

2 Timothy 1:6
Therefore, I remind you to stir up the gift of God, which is in you through the laying on of My hands.

Once you can meditate on His word, renewing your mind, taking on a new way of speaking, and have it in you that your heart is restored the fruits of the spirit start to manifest, and you are filled with everlasting joy. Do you know what the fruits of the spirit are? List them below, if not it is alright, I am going to tell you.

Fruits of the Spirit

- LOVE
- JOY
- PEACE
- PATIENCE
- KINDNESS
- GOODNESS
- FAITHFULNESS
- GENTLENESS
- SELF CONTROL

Galatians 5:22-23
Against such things, there is no law.

As we pour out the fruits of the spirit, we too shall receive Love, Joy, Peace, Patience, Kindness, Goodness, Faithfulness, Gentleness, and self-control in return. I am all for receiving all the above. Some will say "I pour out my love but I don't get it back!" or my favorite "I'm kind but some people are rude". Are you trying to love with the expectation of being loved?

Why do you care how people act especially when they are not walking in alignment with God? You cannot be loving and not kind or kind and not have patience, nor can you pick and choose when you want to pour out God's fruits. God's love, patience, faithfulness amongst all the other fruits are continually given to everyone, for we are all brothers and sisters in the eyes of the Lord and deserve forgiveness.

That reminds me of the book of Jonah the prophet and how he ran from God because God wanted him to visit Nineveh to warn them of God's wrath that would come if they did not stop living in their wicked ways, well Jonah did not think they deserved God's mercy, good grace, or forgiveness. So, he disobeyed God and tried to run, could you imagine trying to run from God?

God eventually got his message across to the Nineveh by Jonah non the less and all were saved, And Jonah learned a lesson or two about God's forgiveness along the way.

If there are fruits that you use or have mastered more than others, encourage yourself to use the fruits you have not mastered this week and allow yourself time to master them, but first write down where you think you need help.

I know when I started this walk my patience and self-control were all over the place, I mean I had little to no tolerance for people, I had road rage, and couldn't stand being held up at the cashier line, you name it I would lose my patience over, and my favorite line was "JESUS TAKE THE WHEEL"!

Those moments God's trying to slow us down believe it or not. He does not need to take the wheel for everything, He gives us the power and authority over all principalities. Now that does not mean He wants us to take on the world without Him, but that He wants us to allow Him to use us, He may be trying to talk to us or wanting us to talk to someone else about salvation or even share a smile, maybe just a kind gesture. Sometimes what would Jesus do was the last thing I thought about, so I had to pray long and hard for this change. I cannot help but laugh now. I am far from perfect, but He is perfection, He walks with me through it all, somedays I still feel like I am going to lose my patience or self-control being a single mom of two boys, one being a teenager and the other a 6-year-old with health deficiencies and behavior disorders had its own trials, and now add working over 50 hours a week. Who wouldn't need a timeout?

Life is hard but it is not impossible with Christ Jesus and God always reminding us He is always in control, He has us covered, he has all things already worked out for our good. We do not need to fret over anything but pray about everything.

Write down what you need to work on here and when your done ask God to help build you up in these areas, now do not be surprised when God hits you with a little of all the things you are trying to grow from at once. Remember your Faith will be tested for it produces patience and with patience, endurance. Do not give up!

Knowing

—⧫⟡⟡⧫—

Romans 8:28
We know that all things work together for good to those who love God, those that are called according to His purpose.

2 Peter 1:5
Make every effort to respond to God's promises,
your faith with a generous provision of this...
- *Moral excellence (virtue)*
- *Knowledge*
- *Self-control*
- *Perseverance*
- *Godliness*
- *Mutual Affection (brotherly love)*
- *Love*

Knowing what that means is important...

Moral excellence: The quality of doing what is right and avoiding what is wrong.

Knowledge: The ability to teach the word, but also with forms of revelation a spiritual gift, the word of wisdom.

Self-Control: Dying to fleshly desires.

Perseverance: To continue in a course of action even in the face of adversity.

Godliness: The practice of conforming to the laws and wishes of God.

Brotherly love: Natural affection toward the greater community of believers/followers.

Love: Is patient and kind, love is not envious or boastful or arrogant or rude. It does not insist on its own way; It is not irritable or resentful, it does not rejoice in wrongdoing but rejoices in the truth.

Gods' promises are always true, *"His word will not return void, but it shall accomplish that which He pleases, and it shall prosper in the thing whereto He sent it,"* as it is said in **Isaiah 55:11**, unlike the word of man that at times it is contradicting or conflicting, and undependable.

God gives us a guide on how He would like us to collaborate with Him in this world according to what is pleasing to Him and His promises for us and we will be prosperous.

I do not know about you, but I get excited thinking... Wow God, you chose ME! God, you love ME! You want ME to help you teach this word to your people. Wow Me? Lord! You chose me before I chose you and you have been here the whole time waiting for me to choose you, protecting me from what the enemy tried to steal from me.

What better love is that? A lot of us spend our entire life longing for unconditional, selfless love and do any oh type of thing looking for it. Not realizing or forgetting God gives it freely unconditionally through the salvation of our Lord Jesus Christ. Do you know what unconditionally means? It means you do not have to do anything to get his love, you do not have to change who you are before He can love you... He loves you! With your flaws He loves you all of you!

God is waiting to pour out His promises unto you. He's like a vault holding blessings and promises just ready to bust open for you. Your commitment to the word of God is the code. Following His guide (the bible) and getting to know Him relationally, His love, having virtue, self-control, choosing Him even when it is difficult, and just doing away with your old ways of thinking and submitting to Godliness behavior. He will pour out the desires of your heart unto you, how awesome is that?

I remember giving my whole self to crappy relationships going through the motions for the sake of "love"! Changing my ways, the way I think and act to try and make someone love me even though they did not appreciate the love I was already pouring out to them by me being myself.

God says do not change for a man. Be renewed in me and through me, for I have loved you, and accept you as you are, healing the brokenness inside you and giving you, your heart's desires, and the blessings you deserve, and my blessings will come without sorrow. All Glory to God! Thank you, Jesus!

I am excited for the renewing going on in you, I am excited for the promise God is about to release unto you, I am excited for how He is about to move on your behalf. I am excited about the works you are going to be doing for the kingdom of God.

Ephesians 4:22
Put off concerning your formal conduct. The old man, which grows corrupt according to the deceitful lust and is renewed in the spirit of your mind, and that you put on the new man which was created according to God in true righteousness and holiness.

Do Not Be Weary!

Galatians 6:9

And let us not grow weary while doing good. For in due season, we shall reap if we do not lose heart.

John 14:27

"Peace I leave with you, my peace I give to you; not as the world gives do I give to you. Let not your heart be troubled neither let it be afraid."

Psalm 27:1

The Lord is my light and my salvation: Whom shall, I fear? The Lord is the strength of my life; of whom shall I be afraid.

Psalms 16 7-9

I will bless the Lord who has given me counsel; My heart also instructs me in the night seasons. I have set the Lord always before me; Because He is at my right hand I shall not be moved. Therefore, my heart is glad, and my glory rejoices, my flesh also rests in hope.

1 Peter 2:12
Having your conduct honorable among the Gentiles, that when they speak against you as evildoers, they may, by your good works which they observe, glorify God in the day of visitation.

Doing what is right and abiding in the word you are going to have to stand firm on to it. Sometimes being confronted by people in disagreement with the teaching of the word or just do not understand. But as Jesus said in **John 4:34** *"My food is to do the will of Him who sent me, and to finish His works."* Remember Jesus paved the way so that we can preach his Father's word without shame, there is nothing we will come against that Jesus did not already face and overcame.

In **John 16:33** He reminds us to *"Be of good cheer, I have overcome the world"*, in **Revelations** *"He who has ears, let him hear what the Spirit says to the churches"*. And in **Isaiah 51**, *"I am he who comforts you. Who are you that you should be afraid of man who will die, and of the son of a man who will be made like grass"*?

You must find comfort in knowing that you are covered and that the word of God will come forth and will not come back void. Why wouldn't you want to share the gospel?

For you are not like the son of man anymore who walks around with no purpose. Like grass, once dead it is dried up and withers to nothing, but you are the sons and daughters of the King and have everlasting life!

John 10:14

I am the good Shepherd; and I know my sheep and am know by my own, "as the Father knows me" even so I know the Father and I lay down my life for the sheep.

He is Unfailing, Unchanging

Galatians 5:16

I say then: walk in the spirit, and you shall not fulfill the lust of the flesh.

James 1:5

If any of you lacks wisdom, let him ask of God, who gives to all liberally and without reproach and it will be given to him.

Hebrews 13:8

Jesus Christ is the same Yesterday, Today, and forever.

Malachi 3:6

For I am the Lord, I will not change.

The Spirit

⬦⬦⬦

Samuel 16:7

But the Lord said to Samuel, do not look at his appearance or at his physical stature, because I have refused him. For the Lord does not see as man sees. For man looks at the outward appearance, but the Lord looks at the heart.

2 Corinthians 4:18

While we do not look at the things which are seen, but at the things which are not seen, for the things which are seen are temporary, but the things which are not seen are eternal.

2 Corinthians 3:17

Now the Lord is the spirit, and where the spirit of the Lord is there is Liberty.

The Holy Spirit lives in us and works through us you need to just abide in His word to activate these spiritual gifts. Unlike salvation, you need not to do works for only have faith that the Lord our God died on the cross for our indiscretions. The gifts of the spirit need your works. The spirit needs you to not only hear the word but accept it, hold on to it, meditate in it day and night, and to live by it then share the gospel, for the word is not for you alone it is for all to hear. When you hear the word, you get a sense of freedom a sense of peace, and of joy, that is liberty. You should want everyone to experience the Lord's liberty. It is important not to allow yourself to be imprisoned spiritually, that is how the Lord speaks through you and can use you.

Are you abiding in His word to hear Him?

What has the Lord been speaking to you about?

What can you be doing better to hear what He is saying to you?

Are you talking over Him and His purpose for you?

Abiding

Proverbs 13:3
He who guards his mouth preserves his life, but he who opens wide his lips shall have destruction.

Proverbs 10:22
The Blessing of the Lord makes one rich, and he adds no sorrow with it.

John 14:15
"If you love me, keep my commandments and I will pray for the father and He will give you another helper, that He may abide with you forever. "The spirit of truth. Whom the world cannot receive because it neither sees Him nor knows Him. But you know Him for He dwells with you & will be in you "I will not leave you orphans; I will come to you.

Psalms 37:39
But the Salvation of the righteous is from the Lord, He is their strength in the time of trouble, and the Lord shall help them and deliver them from the wicked and save them because they trust in Him.

Psalms 3:3
You, oh Lord, are a shield for me, my glory, and the one who lifts my head. I cried to the Lord with my voice, and He heard me from His holy Hill.

Psalms 5: 11-12
But let all those rejoice who put their trust in you. Let them ever shout your joy. Because you defend them, let those also who love your name be joyful in you. For you, O Lord will bless the righteous with favor. You will surround Him, as with a shield.

I want you to take this time to reflect on the verses just given to you about abiding, there are moments in life where we question what we are facing in life and God's presence in what we are going through. Rest sure with these verses that He is with you, and He is guarding you like a shield, He will hear you when you cry out to Him.

How many times have we read that He will not only hear us, but He walks with us and guards us through all life's circumstances?

Did you know there are 365 verses of "Fear Nots" scriptures, which means there is a verse for every day we come against trials?

God wants us to remember that we are not alone He understands and knows there will be trials and we are going to be tested but He wants to know what are you going to do during that time of the test?

What kind of soil are you going to be? In the book of Mark chapter 4, Jesus gave a parable to the people about the sower going out to sow...

as he sowed seeds some fell on some rocky ground where it did not have much soil, so it immediately sprung up but because of the lack of soil there were no roots, so when the sun came out it burned it up and it withered away...

Some seed fell among thorns. And the Thorns grew up and choked it. And there were no crops.

But the other seeds well they fell on good soil. And grew, great crops that sprung up an increased and produced, and multiplied some 30-fold, some 60-fold, and some 100-fold.

What kind of soil are you?

Do you hear the word then hit a rocky place and let your faith die out?

Do you hear the word, accept it but your faith is easily moved or choked up by your trials?

What are you doing to be good soil?

What are you doing to produce?

What verses help to encourage you to be good soil?

We are farmers of the word we cannot allow someone's bad harvest or weeds to affect the way we move in faith. Remember everything works out together for the good of those who love God and are called. We should not be moved, is anything too hard for Him?

Prayer time:

with *Hebrews 13:20-21*

Now may the Lord of Peace, who brought up our Lord Jesus from the dead, that great Shepherd of the sheep, through the blood of the everlasting covenant, make you complete in every good work to do His will, working in you what is well pleasing in his sight, through Jesus Christ, to whom be glory forever and ever, Amen.

Write down your own prayer or add to this prayer here...

Check Yourself

1 Corinthians 11:28-31

But let a man examine himself, and so let him eat of the bread and drink of the cup, for he who eats and drinks in an unworthy manner, eats and drinks judgment to himself. Not discerning (being aware of) the Lord's body. For this reason, many are weak and sick among you, and many sleep, for if we would judge ourselves. We would not be judged.

Daniel 11:32

Those who do wickedly against the Covenant, he shall corrupt with flattery, but the people who know their God shall be strong and carry out great exploits.

Proverbs 11:25

The generous soul will be made rich, and he who waters will also be watered himself.

Deuteronomy 24:19

When you reap your harvest in your field and forget a sheaf in the field you shall not go back to get it, it shall be for the stranger, the fatherless, and the widow. That the Lord your God may bless you in all the work, of your hands.

2 Chronicles 7:14
If my people who are called by my name will humble themselves,
pray and seek my face, and turn from their wicked ways. Then I will
hear from heaven and will forgive their sin and heal their land.

1 Chronicle 4:10
Jabez called on the God of Israel, saying, "that you would bless me
indeed. And enlarge my territory that your hand would be with
me, and you would keep me from evil, that I may not cause pain."
So, God granted him what he requested.

Humbling yourselves is not just about not bragging when you
have money or material blessings. Humbling yourself is giving
your whole self to Gods will for your life, not giving in to selfish
desires or doing things for eye service, it is giving yourself completely to God, submitting your soul, your mind and not dis-
honoring your body, doing so without boasting in oneself but
boasting in the Lord. Giving unto the poor, widowed, and
elderly without swaggering unless it is to give God the glory.
Humbling yourself requires asking forgiveness with repentance
and when God searches your heart He can tell if you are sincere
in your humbling or just seeking to be seen.

There is not much written about Jabez and His life, but I could
imagine given a name that is described to mean "he makes sor-
rowful" and the fact that he felt he needed to humble himself
before the Lord and pray this prayer in 1 chronicle helps me to
believe that life was not easy for him, and he was struggling but
knew God was the answer. When he prayed God sought out

his heart and granted his request. God is faithful and His love endures forever. God genuinely wants the best for His children and His plan is good for us, He only asks that we give up living by the flesh and humble ourselves to Him.

Have you seen the show "Hoarders"? If you have not, I am sure you could imagine or even know one. Hoarders are known as people with a mental disorder who collect or buy too much of the same item and do not throw anything away and usually hide it from people because they typically do not live acceptably. Now imagine your body being the dwelling place and you are the hoarder, consuming drinks, smoking, unmarried sexual encounters sometimes with multiple people, eating unclean foods, or just binge eating, emotional hoarders not just sad emotions but anger, hurt, selfishness, pride, hoarding traumatic experiences.

Would you want to live inside your body with all this surrounding you? How could you expect God to, and want Him to work in you or do works through you? You cannot work in an unstable environment, but you expect God to? I am not saying He cannot work with you; I am saying how efficient can He be when you are giving in to your fleshly desires. You're asking for forgiveness and then fighting against Him, you're giving to the needy but boasting about it, you're praising Him for blessings but spending it on alcohol and or drugs or going places you shouldn't be associated with, you are crying out for His help but then reacting emotionally when your moved by a situation or going back to the situations that made you unstable, you're fighting against Him and expecting life-changing results,

2 chronicles; *"If my children who are called by my name will humble themselves, pray and seek my face turn from their wicked ways, then I will hear from heaven and forgive them and heal their land,"* it is all about humbling yourself and submitting to Him daily. It is not easy, but it is not impossible because God cannot fail. *Greater is he who is in us than he who is in the world.* Meditate in His word day and night so you can resist the devil.

What habits or disorders or traumas has the enemy placed in your life that make you feel defeated?

I want to take this time to Pray with you,

Dear heavenly Father I put my trust in you, let me never be put to shame again, deliver me from the evil one in your righteousness and cause me to escape ("fill in the blank with the above list ") incline your ear to me and save me, for you are my strong tower and refuge to which I may resort in my time of need, fill me with the Holy Spirit that gives direction and discernment today, I ask that you continue to direct my path and allow me to discern your truth over the enemies lies, show me how I should move today expose the enemies lies heavenly father, thank you for forgiving me of my sins the ones known and the ones unknown I ask that you continue to purify my mind my heart my spirit and my soul. I'm asking you to remove anything that is not like you, I want to be used by you Lord I pray this in your mighty name Jesus. Amen

He is Faithful

⟣⟢∘⟡⟐⟡∘⟣⟢

Luke 11:9
So, I say to you, Ask and it will be given to you, seek and you will find; Knock and it shall be opened to you.

Matthew 6:33
Seek the kingdom of God above all else, and live righteously, and He will give you everything you need.

Hebrews 10:24
Let us think of ways to motivate one another to acts of love and good works.

Romans 12:10
Love each other with genuine affection and take delight in honoring each other.

Colossians 3:14
Above all clothe yourselves with love, which binds us all together in perfect harmony.

Galatians 6:2
Share each other's burdens and in this way obey the law of Christ.

Ecclesiastes 4:10
If one person falls the other can reach out and help, but someone who falls alone is in real trouble.

Ephesians 4:3
Make every effort to keep yourselves united in the spirit, Binding yourselves together with peace.

Ecclesiastes 4:9
Two people are better off than one, for they can help each other succeed.

Matthew 18:20
For where two or three are gathered as my followers, I am there among them.

Colossians 3:23
Work willing at whatever you do, as though you were working for the Lord rather than for people. Remember that the lord will give you an inheritance as your reward and that the master you are serving is Christ.

Rather we are together going through trials or alone we should, like in **Romans 5:3** *"Rejoice in those problems for we know that they help develop endurance."* But God does not want us to battle alone, subsequently, He puts in our path a fellowship family of like-minded people to go and pray through those trials with you. Do not worry yourself with the things of the moment for God promises that those things are just for a season, and this too shall pass. Instead, let the Spirit renew your thoughts and attitudes, put on your new nature created to be like God-truly righteous and holy. *Ephesians 4:23-24*

Make a list of like-minded brethren you call on, in a time of need in prayer or advice it is important to know your circle...

Romans 12:2
And now, dear brothers and sisters one final thing fix your thoughts on what is true, and honorable and right and pure and lovely and admirable. Think about things that are excellent and worthy of praise.

Verses to Meditate

Isaiah 26:3
You will keep in perfect peace all who trust in you, all whose thoughts are fixed on you.

Matthew 20:28
For even the son of man came not to be served but to serve others and give his life as a ransom.

Ephesians 3:20
Now all glory to God, who is able through his mighty power at work within us to accomplish infinitely more than we might ask or think.

Matthew 5:14
You are the light of the world like a city on a hilltop that cannot be hidden.

Romans 12:21
Do not let evil conquer you but conquer evil by doing good.

Colossians 3:2
Think about the things of heaven, not the things of earth.

2 Corinthians 10:5
We destroy every proud obstacle that keeps people from knowing
God. We capture their rebellious thoughts and teach them to
obey Christ.

There comes a time when you are going to face battles and you
will not understand why. You're going to want to question your
faith, question when is God going to show off his muscle, even
ask yourself what more can you do? sometimes it has nothing
to do with what you're doing but what others deserve and they
don't deserve you or you think to yourself what are you not
doing, and honestly, the truth is it's just going to take more time
for certain things to work itself out. Not because God's miracles
are running low, or you have not prayed enough or prayed the
right words, and your faith is always enough. God just needs
you to wait this one out and this is when your patience gets
tried the most at least for me especially after God has given me
a word, and confirmation. I find myself talking to God saying,
"okay I am ready for its God hands wide open". Then you hear
God say be still, "wait". Who wants to hear that right?

Just like a child that wants something that fell while driving, but
you know even if you manage to reach it and get it, they might
drop it again because you are moving, and the car is moving, also
the child's hands are moving and not to mention you can cause
an accident if you take your eyes off the road for one second,
or take a wrong turn leading to a detour. Meanwhile, you are
thinking we are going someplace that is going to take your mind

off that little old thing, and it is so much bigger and better, so, your advice to your impatient child is "be patience, wait"!

How would that work out for you? Like my child probably, cry and struggle to reach for it themselves only becoming more frustrated, hurt, and irritable, waiting for you to get to a point that they can safely receive it. Well God's that parent trying to drive us through our life's choices making sure everything is safe and we are in a safe place, before he can give us a blessing, he is ready to hand us, he wants to make sure all mirrors are clear of any possible detours or accidents that we may have ran into in the past. So, waiting does not always mean no! It just means not yet, not right now, but even if it is a no, that is okay understand that even if it is a no from God what He has in store for you is going to exceed your expectation every time, and we are just reaching too low, like a distraction that has fallen that we keep trying to pick up.

Taking Out the Garbage

Ephesians 4:31-32
Get rid of all bitterness, rage, and anger, brawling and slander along with every form of malice be kind and compassionate to one another, forgiving each other just as God in Christ forgave you.

Matthew 5:44
But I say to you love your enemies bless those who curse you, do good to those who spitefully use you and persecute you.

Matthew 6:24
No one can serve two masters for either he will hate the one and love the other or else he will be loyal to the one and despise the other you cannot serve God and wealth.

Philippians 4:19-20
And my God shall supply all your needs according to His riches and glory by Christ Jesus. To our God & Father be the glory forever.

Ephesians 4:25-28
Therefore, putting away lying "let each one of you speak with truth with his neighbor," for we are members of one another. Be angry and do not sin, do not let the sun go down on your wrath. Nor give

place for the devil. Let him who stole steal no more, but rather let him labor, working with his hands what is good that he may have something to give him who has need.

Ephesians 3:30
Do not grieve the holy spirit of God.

People will disappoint you which will lead to different emotions depending on the situation, but God wants us to forgive and replace those feelings with prayer and words of edification, if you cannot find the words to speak then remain quiet and ask God for peace over the circumstances, you are facing for God in Christ Jesus has forgiven us so that we can forgive others. Easy to say at first but with prayer it does get easier once you get a taste of that love, joy, peace that God offers there is nothing you are going to allow to disturb that. So before lashing out being bitter or angry, curse them or go to bed with wrath in your heart pray about everything disturbing your spirit.

Also, God will supply ALL of our needs so do not preoccupy yourself with the wealth that comes from man for often it is temporary and far too often it does not bring true happiness or peace. Like a song, I listen to by Mase, back in my worldly life stated "more money more problems" that is because most times people idolize money, and you cannot serve God and mammon. For all these things give place for the devil to work grieving the Holy Spirit of God.

Are there some things you have allowed yourself to obsess over in anger, bitterness, or money?

Have you felt the Holy Spirit grieved but do not understand why? Ask God to expose where the enemy is lying to you.

Are there some people you need to forgive? Place their names here as if you are releasing the situation or circumstances to God and let God have his way with it.

There is nothing weak about walking away from negative conditions and allowing God to have His way with it emotionally, physically, and or financially for we are called for His purpose, and He will not allow us to suffer if we walk in the spirit of God with us. So, take out the garbage that has a stronghold over you right now. You are enough, you are incredible, you are chosen to do great things and are called for His purpose. Fear not! Remember there is a verse for every day of the year you come across fear.

Listen

Philippians 4:8-9

Finally, brethren

- *whatever things are true*
- *whatever things are noble*
- *whatever things are just*
- *whatever things are pure*
- *whatever things are lovely*
- *whatever things are of good report*

if there is any virtue and if there is anything praiseworthy meditate on these things which you learned and received and heard and saw in me these do and the God of peace will be with you.

John 14:6

Jesus said to him, I am the way, the truth, and the life. No one comes to the Father except through me.

Psalms 145:8-9

The Lord is gracious and full of compassion, slow to anger, and great in mercy. The Lord is good to all, and His mercies are over all His works.

John 13:20
Most assuredly, I say to you he who receives whomever I send, receives Me; and he who receives Me receives Him who sent me.

Psalms 27:13
I would have lost heart unless I had believed that I would see the goodness of the Lord in the land of the living.

Meditate on all things true, noble, just, pure, lovely, and of good report. This is so important when we are living in a culture that praises bad behavior, poor attitude, disrespect, and selfishness. Knowingly or not, you get what you put out. If you live a life abiding by the culture, that we live in today you only have yourself to blame for the wickedness that you receive back from worldly culture. God gave His son Jesus Christ so we can receive Him and all the glory that comes with serving Him; salvation, love, peace, joy, and life abundantly greater than we could ever imagine. The Lord is full of compassion and grace, and His mercies are forever given. But our culture tries to teach us that forgiving and being compassionate; are weak, and carrying around anger, hate, and unforgiveness is strength.

With Jesus it's the complete opposite, he said, *"I am the truth and the life. And no one gets to the Father but through me"*. Who is stronger than the Father, the Son and Holy Spirit?

Again, in **John 13:20** he states, *"I say to you, he who receives whoever I send receives Me; And he who receives Me receives Him who sent Me."* I am glad that I received Him. And like in ***Psalms***

69

27:13; "*I would have lost heart unless I believed that I would see the goodness of the Lord in this world.*" I improvised here a little, but it resonated to my life at the time I was ready to give up. I thought my old life was it! I was stoned, medicated, and drinking most of the time, with little-to- no motivation to find my purpose. I battled manic depression, bipolar disorder, and anxiety, but thought I had it all under control, according to culture's view. I mean, I wasn't lashing out-, or taking it out on anyone, but myself. Most people would have never known or could tell I had a problem, but typically, the people no one suspects are the ones suffering the most.

Honestly, I thought I was finished. I had reached the "this is as good as it's going to get" stage, but the Godly spirit that was instilled in me since a young age would not let me give up there. Once I submitted myself to God, and distanced myself from a toxic relationship, and a toxic environment, I found that God started to move expeditiously on my behalf. He was moving mountains. At that point. I decided I wanted to go deeper into His word. I wanted to grow deeper in my relationship with Him. I wanted more of His grace and mercy but most importantly, I wanted and needed His love. I went on a fast, and at that moment God, gave me the strength to give up my addictions. I have not needed to take any medications for depression, or any disorders, since. I used to suffer from severe migraines and had to take medications for that as well, but not anymore. All glory be to God, and that was just the beginning. I would have lost heart had I not received my Lord and believed that I would see more of Gods miraculous works.

Where do want to see God move in your life?

Be a Witness

John 14:27

"Peace I leave with you the peace I give to you, not as the world gives do I give to you. Let not your heart be troubled, neither let it be afraid."

Mark 16:20

And they went out and preached everywhere, the Lord working with them and confirming the word through the accompanying signs.
Amen

John 14:13-14

And whatever you ask in my name, That I will do, that the Father may be glorified in the son. You may ask anything in my name, and I will do it.

1 Peter 3:15

But sanctify the Lord God in your hearts, and always be ready to give a defense to everyone who asks you a reason for the hope that is in you. With meekness and fear, having a good conscience that when they defame you as evildoers, those who revile your good care conduct in Christ may be ashamed.

Your calling is much greater than what people outside the will of God's view of you may be, or what anyone has to say about you. You are called to be a witness of His goodness, His mercy, and His grace. You are called according to His perfect will.

Your Forever Partner

<hr/>

John 16:25

Holy Spirit will bring in your remembrance all that I have said.

Acts 1:8

But you shall receive power when the Holy Spirit has come upon you, and you shall be witnesses to me in Jerusalem. And in all Judea and Samaria, and to the end of the earth.

Galatians 6:8

Whoever sows to please their flesh, from the flesh will reap destruction; whoever sows to please the spirit, from the spirit will reap eternal life.

Luke 12:2-3

For there is nothing covered that will not be revealed, nor hidden that will not be known. "Therefore, whatever you have spoken in the dark will be heard in the light and what you have spoken in the ear in inner rooms will be proclaimed on the housetops."

Galatians 5:17
For the flesh lust against the spirit and the spirit against the flesh, and these are contrary to one another so that you so not do the thing that you wish.

Galatians 5:19-21
Now the works of the flesh, are evident which are adultery, fornication, uncleanliness lewdness, idolatry, sorcery, hatred, contentions, jealousy outburst of wrath, selfish ambition, dissensions, heresies, envy, murders, drunkenness, revelries, and the like of which, I tell you beforehand just as I also told you in past times that those who practice such things will not inherit the Kingdom of God

John 3:5-6
Jesus answered, "Most assuredly I say to you unless one is born of water and the spirit. He cannot enter the Kingdom of God. That which is born of the flesh is flesh, and that which is born of the spirit is spirit."

1 Peter 2:9
But you are not like that, for you are chosen people you are Royal priests, a holy nation. God's very own possession. As a result, you can show others the goodness of God for he called you out of the darkness into wonderful light.

2 Corinthians 5:17
This means that anyone who belongs to Christ Jesus has become a new person. The old life is gone; a new life has begun!

The Holy Spirit is an amazing gift that helps your relational wholeness with our Lord Jesus Christ. It is an outstanding feeling to be baptized by water, but the baptism of the Holy Spirit is unmeasurable in comparison. The Holy Spirit comes upon you by faith it is a gift given to everyone but very few exercise this gift. The thought of most, is you must be some grand person or someone perfect but that is a lie from the pits of hell. The Holy Spirit is freely given to all who have faith in our Lord Jesus Christ. It is the way God communicates with you in different measures and it is so beautiful and so amazing. I will go as far as to say it is one of the most precious gifts you will ever receive.

John 1:12
To all who believe in Him and accepted Him, he gave the right to become children of God.

What do children receive when they become of age or the passing of a relative? **"Inheritance"**

Our Lord Jesus Christ has already died. Giving up His life for us as a sacrifice to God the Father and creator of all things, for our sins so we can inherit the kingdom. Not only to receive the salvation of God but to also receive the inheritance, we only need to become of mature age meaning relational wholeness. Everyone's age is different when they become relationally whole with Christ and receive their inheritance. Most of us must go through some trials due to our life's decisions but then we are able to be a witness and testimony for someone else's life so they can find their purpose for the Kingdom of God.

Meditation Notes

What are your thoughts? How do you feel? Are you already feeling Holy Spirit-Filled? Having dreams or visions? It is important to write down these types of things and talk to God about what they mean. Use this space for yourself.

Give God Glory!

Romans 11:36
For of him and through him and to him are all thing to whom be glory forever.
Amen

John 8:31-32
"If you abide in my word, you are my disciples I indeed and you shall know the truth shall make you free."

Being a disciple:

- Live by the word – Do not give anyone reason to say you are not a follower of Jesus Christ by the way you live.

- Spread the word – Be spreaders of the word, talk to people about the word of God, and Christ Jesus.

- Carriers of the word – Wherever you go, whatever circumstances you come against carrying the word, speak to your situation from what God has told you according to the word.

Daniel 10:12
Then He said to me; "Do not fear, Daniel for from the first day that you set your heart to understand and to humble. Yourself before your God, your words were heard, I have come because of your words."

Matthew 6:34
Therefore, do not worry about tomorrow for tomorrow will worry about its own things, sufficient for the day is its own trouble.

Less Self

Proverbs 3:7
Do not be wise in your own eye fear the word and depart from evil.
It will be health to your flesh, and strength to your bones.

Romans 8:6
To Be carnally minded is death but to be spiritually minded is life and peace.

Luke 18:14
For everyone who exalts himself will be humbled and he who humbles himself will be exalted.

James 1:26
If anyone among you thinks he is religious and does not bridle his tongue but deceives his own heart this one's religion is useless.

Matthew 25:13
"Watch therefore, for you know neither the day nor the hour in which the son of man is coming."

Proverbs 6:16-19
These six things the Lord hates, yes seven are an abomination to him.

1. A proud look

2. A lying tongue

3. Hands that shed innocent blood

4. A heart that devises wicked plans.

5. Feet that are swift in funning to evil.

6. A false witness who speaks lies.

7. One who sows discord among brethren.

In a "Dog eat Dog" culture it is difficult to know when you are or if you are being selfless but following the Lord's commandments, is a sure way to build up the Holy Spirit to guide you through this worlds wickedness and bring others to the same salvation you have found. When you are in a situation that seems trying, difficult, and unchanging, first, write down the matter of the difficult/unchanging situation...

Ask yourself am I looking at this with less of me and more of God's thought process?

Or am I tired of dealing with it and ready for it to be moved either way not willing to learn from it?

Is there anything you can change about the situation/circumstances from a Godly perspective? How?

Remember some things will arise and or keep arising until you deal with them following God's plan. (LESS OF YOU, MORE OF HIM) Do not think you are above anyone else because you are now walking with Christ, we are all called according to His purpose. Remember that some followers are not where you are spiritually, and it is important that we are continually humbling ourselves in the "Flesh" and looking at every circumstance with a Godly point view.

Just as any parent God has given us rules to follow, a word to live by, and things to do, but above all else, He gives us a view of the things He hates most of the flesh. So, there is no mistake when you start to abide by the will of the Lord, your held accountable for when your called to God on judgement day and He presents you with your life's chore list, of situations and circumstances, that you came across. How did you address it? Were you being proud, Lying, shedding innocent blood, being deceitful with wicked plans or plots, running quickly to evil instead, or being a false witness speaking lies for yourself or someone else, and more so did you bring problems amongst those considered to be your brethren in Christ Jesus?

What is on your chore list that you still need to work on?

Do not be discouraged by these things! We live in a flesh ran culture, and we all fall short of God's glory, we are not perfect but with Him "Christ Jesus" and through him we can accomplish anything and get through anything. Remembering that it is about selflessness, not selfishness, that we are all saved and forgiven.

He Chose Us

2 Peter 1:1-2
To those who through the righteousness of our God and Savior Jesus Christ have received a faith as precious as ours; grace and peace be yours in abundance through the knowledge of God and Jesus our Lord.

1 Timothy 4:12
Let no one despise your youth, but be an example to the believers in word, in conduct, in love in spirit, in faith, in purity.

Romans 14:8
For if we live to the Lord and if we die, we die to the Lord, therefore whether we live or die we are the Lords.

About the Author

I'm Elisha Perez of Lancaster Pa, born in the 80's when it was cultures norm to practice drug use, and with music and dancing being most individuals way of coping with their life. My parents were no exception. I was an outsider in my own surroundings, and never felt completely comfortable anywhere. Continually battling mental, physical, and sexual abuse, it wasn't easy believing God was my salvation for many years, no matter how much word my grandmother instilled in me as a child. Life's evils seem a lot bigger than God's purpose for my life hence me in and out of church my whole life. My spirit however longed for something more, but my flesh didn't want me to believe I was worth more.

I am a woman of God, a lifelong student of the word, a messenger of the Lord Jesus Christ, disguised as a medical assistant, single mother of two wonderful children, a creature of creativity, makeup enthusiast and cosmetologist. I love to laugh and bring joy and laughter to those around me. Nothing brings me more joy then cooking for people, feeding them not only food but spiritual knowledge of the Lord. I love being outdoors adoring God's creation the ocean is probably my favorite place; it reminds me of how grand and big God does His works. I am from Pennsylvania there isn't too many bodies of water around. So, when I moved to Florida it felt like a refreshing transformation, little did I know it would be more of a complete restoration of my life. A journey it had been. I struggled with drugs and alcohol trying to numb up life circumstances. Had I allowed the enemy to have his way only Lord knows where I would be, if becoming an author, leading people to the salvation of our Lord Jesus Christ would have come to pass. What I do know is that my story is just beginning. Our God saves, He restores, renews but most importantly He loves, and He chooses to love us every day, with just a step out of the dark place into a new place called faith He gives us a purpose filled life, and in every day, there is a chance to make it beautiful and be led by your purpose.

I am not perfect, I am learning every day just like you, we are all students in this school of life, but I get to choose my teacher. I am learning how to follow the Lord's lead, He who saves and restores, and He who is a strong foundation and fortress for us all. I will sing His praises, bless His Holy name, and share the gospel as long as I shall live. My name is Elisha and I love you and remember first Jesus loved you, this book is for the lost but never forgotten. God chose you for such a time as this. You are in my prayers. God Bless you.

Thank you

CPSIA information can be obtained
at www.ICGtesting.com
Printed in the USA
LVHW070147011021
699020LV00032B/1355